M000198564

THE DAY I MET
BIGFOOT

BY CRAIG DURHAM

To Kimberley.

THE DAY I MET BIGFOOT

CONTENTS

THE DAY I MET BIGFOOT

CHAPTER 1

WHO AM I?

"**D**o you ever stop and think about how small we are in the universe?" I say this to Kenny as we stare into the dark moonlit sky. It's about 2am, we are resting up against some trees on our makeshift hammock. Exhausted and freezing we begin to discuss what our next move should be. We had just ran from what was possibly another Bigfoot or a bear. It wasn't long after running away that we had found ourselves lost in the woods. After the experience we had earlier in the day with a Bigfoot we knew anything could happen now and unfortunately we were barely prepared to survive the night.

My mind was racing and Kenny and I were talking so much that I hardly slept at all that night. We may have eventually dozed off for a minute or two but that's about it. Our whole life changed in an instant earlier that day and I think we were just starting to grasp it all...

That was an interesting night about twenty years ago and now after all this time I still find myself lying in bed re-living that life changing event. Although reluctant and after some coercing from a co-worker I figured why not tell this story. I've thought about doing it before and wondered if anyone would listen, and if anyone even cares, I suppose you'll understand later on in the story why.

I think I decided to write this book because this is not just a story about Bigfoot. It's about the friends and family that are involved. This book is primarily for them but I'm grateful for anyone else who takes their time to read it.

Most of this story takes place in about one week but overall it spans roughly the past twenty years. I believe this story is a truly incredible adventure that my childhood friend Kenny and I experienced some years ago while on vacation.

I have told this story to many people throughout the years who probably thought that I was either nuts or perhaps I just had some wild imagination.

I will give you some background information on myself and the other people involved early on in this story. Information that I believe is necessary to understand how things progressed up until the encounter. This story will include my trip from Boston to California that Kenny and I had taken.

I will mention quickly some of the areas we visited along the way. I want you to understand that the trip started off normal, just as any vacation might. Although in the end this trip later turned out to be one of the craziest and most memorable vacations we could ever imagine. Till this day we appreciate the incredible experience that we will never forget, or want to for that matter.

My story takes place roughly twenty years ago in 1998. It's been awhile so I wanted to write this in a way that I can sit down, concentrate, recall the details, speak with some of the people involved and get the information down from start to finish. I know from the title alone there will be some skeptics and that's ok. I am not out to make anyone a Bigfoot believer. After all these years I know we are lucky enough to have witnessed what we saw. I'm not out to prove anything, I just want to tell my story as we remember it. We have generally kept this to ourselves other than telling a few friends and family. After many years and some convincing from friends I suppose it's time to share my experience.

Since that vacation I have done some research on Bigfoot encounters and sightings around the country. Anyone that is familiar with the famous Bluff Creek footage will know about the debate on sightings being real or fake and well, credibility in this field is often dubious. I understand Bigfoot is right up there in the UFO and paranormal realm. I think that only someone with any sort of interest in the subject gives it a second thought. Typically, it's just a jokey or laughable topic, and that's probably why we have mostly kept it to ourselves.

I remember not too long ago listening to the story of a man who talked about how he lived with a Bigfoot family. He also talked about how he and Bigfoot would enter different dimensions, travel through time and all sorts of nonsense that just puts a bad taste in the mouths of real Bigfoot believers. Yes, I said it, real Bigfoot believers, there is definitely people out there who truly believe. Some may have had encounters like myself or perhaps they just love the idea of a wild man living out there in the woods. Perhaps they just love the folklore, and of course the stories can be fascinating to say the least.

So where do I fit in? Well in this subject I really don't. My name is Craig, I live in Boston, Massachusetts and as you would probably assume we do not have many Bigfoot sightings around the Boston area. At least none that I am aware of anyway.

I should also mention that I am not a Bigfoot Buff or a Bigfoot chaser or anything like that. Although perhaps I am a buff more so now then in 1998 when this whole thing started. In fact, in 1998 I don't think I felt one way or another about Bigfoot. I don't know if I believed it or not. I most likely never thought twice about it.

My only experience with Bigfoot at that time in my life was probably "Harry and the Henderson's." The movie.

So why is it that I say I don't fit in? Well I'm not searching for Bigfoot. I do not go to seminars and do speeches. I am not trying to come up with some crazy convoluted story like hunting and finding Bigfoot and then storing it in my freezer in the garage. Didn't somebody claim that? I also do not collect Bigfoot castings or hair samples. Not that there is anything wrong with searching for Bigfoot, I'm all for it, it's just some of the stories I've heard are pretty farfetched. I take what I know and then compare it to the apparent 4th dimensional intergalactic time traveling Bigfoots out there and maybe you can understand why I haven't been so quick to join that crowd. I'm definitely not out for any Bigfoot limelight. At this point you might be saying "He's writing a book," yes I am, this book however, is probably more for me. For me to tell my story and to sort of re-live the event and remember the friends and family involved.

As you will see there is more to this story than just the encounter with Bigfoot. However, that event does play a pivotal role in who I am today and why I felt this story is one to be told. I would also like to pass down this story to my kids one day. Perhaps there is also someone out there with a similar story, maybe this will encourage them to share their experience as well.

Some of you will believe, some of you just may want to believe but still think it's made up, others will call it a hoax or a joke and that is all fine with me. By now I have accepted all forms of reception. I am not an author, I am not a storyteller I am just a regular guy with a normal life. Outside of that I am just someone who just happened to have had this incredible experience at one time in the woods. It was totally unexpected; however, it was life altering to say the least. I could probably try to go back and recreate the event a thousand times and it would almost certainly never happen again. I believe this is a once in a lifetime experience and I thank you for coming along for the ride.

In case you're not too familiar with Bigfoot here is what I do know. I am not an expert by any stretch of the imagination but I have learned a few things in the years that followed.

Bigfoot lives all around the world. It is thought to be a cross between a human and an ape. Perhaps some split in the evolution of man that branched off. There are many different species and names for Bigfoot that span the entire globe. For example, Russia has the Almas, the Himalayas have the Yeti. The Mande Barung is from India, the list goes on and on. Sasquatch, also known as Bigfoot is from the Pacific-Northwest region of North America. Stories of ancient legend and folklore go back thousands of years.

I mention the Yeti and others to illustrate there are many different names for the Bigfoot related species in almost every continent. I do find it interesting how stories from all around the world have developed thousands of years ago before any forms of modern communication.

All these stories have something that closely resembles some form of a Bigfoot. For myself however I am really only familiar with the American Bigfoot I have seen. I will talk about the behaviors I witnessed and the environment the incident took place in.

I hope you will stick with me until the end because this was an absolutely fascinating time and also an eye opening experience as a human to know that there is obviously so much more about this planet, this world, and the environment that we don't know about, or could possibly understand.

I believe now that these legends and myths are created for a reason, at some point in history some people from an ancient time must have seen a Bigfoot, and they told their stories as well. They were probably made fun of for telling their story too, like people are today.

Nevertheless, throughout history these stories spread all around the world.

And so... The legend of Bigfoot was born...

CHAPTER 2

1998

Over the next several chapters I will tell you about some of my friends and family. Some of the history growing up, my hobbies and some of the events that would lead up to my encounter with Bigfoot. I do feel some of this information is relevant for you to understand how things progressed I believe it will all make sense in the end.

Initially let me say that before all this, I always hated when people said "everything happens for a reason." Well in this case they may be right, the timing and the turn of events that follow my encounter really had a lasting effect on us, the girl I love and how I look at things today in life.

What I have also learned from this is, if you have the means to do what you want to do in life, even the simple things on a daily basis such as going for a bike ride with a friend or calling that person you haven't talked to in years, you should do it because you never know what's going to happen out there. Take time to spend with friends and family because life can be short and you should let things happen naturally, let life guide you in its own way and hopefully it is a great ride. Now with that said let's get on with it.

It is 1998 and I just graduated from high school. At this time my good buddy Kenny and I hang out almost every day. We do not exactly do anything very productive other than a part time job we both occasionally work at and well, we also do a ton of mountain bike riding. We used to skateboard a lot as well but in the past few years mountain biking was our go to for some daily excitement. I had recently broken up with my girlfriend and Kenny was not seeing anyone at that time so we were both pretty busy with the mountain bikes.

There is a densely wooded area right near the neighborhood we both live in. This area had excellent trails that went on for miles and miles. In these woods you could see a deer from time to time and perhaps some squirrels, but that was about it as far as wildlife goes. This area did not exactly prepare us for what was to come. These woods I have to say are lovely, especially in the New England fall and spring time. The temperature is just right and it is a great place to enjoy the outdoors away from city life and traffic.

Kenny and I spent our entire lives in these woods.

Growing up we would ride our BMX bikes down to one of the ponds that was close by and we would catch snapping turtles, frogs and crayfish. We would catch just about anything we could find in there. In the winter time everyone was down there playing ice hockey as well.

I will never forget the time as young kids we had caught this enormous snapping turtle that we brought back to Kenny's house. We let it loose in his backyard. When his father came out back to see what was going on he stepped into the yard while smoking a cigarette, he then threw the cigarette into the grass unaware that there was a snapping turtle on the ground. The turtle snaps at the cigarette and bites down on it. Sure enough it was the right side out and the turtle looked like it was smoking a cigarette. It was hilarious and we all laughed. Later that day we brought the turtle over to my yard. I had an enclosed area that the turtle could walk around in. I only lived a few houses down the street. I suppose we were planning to keep it as a pet. Lugging that turtle around in a five-gallon bucket probably wasn't the best idea either. I think back now and we were great at catching things like frogs, turtles etc... We weren't that great at keeping anything alive. Then again I do recall we would bring most of what we caught back to the pond and release it back into the wild.

It was probably the next day that we noticed the turtle we had caught appeared to be dead, so we decided to bury it out in my backyard. We had buried it in the dirt between a bush and my garage. We also made a grave site for him and added a small wooden cross. We never harmed animals, we actually loved animals. Kenny was always the type to have snakes as pets along with frogs, fish, and dogs. I grew up with cats, fish, dogs, rabbits myself so believe me we always had the best intentions for what we caught.

After we buried the turtle it was possibly the next day when I was out in my backyard that I had noticed the turtle's head was poking through the dirt. We had buried the turtle alive and it was certainly trying to crawl out. I will tell you we both felt awful, we were just young kids excited to catch anything from the pond. Like I said we were not exactly knowledgeable as to what to do with anything after we caught it that was clearly evident.

So fast forward some years later and we still spent most of our time in these same woods but doing a ton of mountain biking. It was the late 90's and a new bike store had opened up. The sport was starting to blow up in popularity and we were both hooked on it as well.

One of our best friends Greg was also big into mountain biking. Sometimes we would hop in Greg's old 1986 battleship grey Dodge Ram pick-up truck and travel around looking for places to go for bike rides. Greg was a couple years older than Kenny and I and he was the only one that had a vehicle we could transport our bikes in. So when Greg came riding we would toss the bikes in the bed of his truck and go exploring all around New England.

We would travel to areas like the woods of Maine and just simply pull off the road looking for trails. There were no smart phone apps to look for trails on the fly like there is today so we had to just wing it. When possible we did have some trail maps we printed off of the computer. If we were lucky enough to find an entrance to a park area or the forest entry there might also be a trail map available that we could use. For the most part though, we really didn't care and we would just hop out of the truck and start riding. I have to say, man oh man did we find some gorgeous places along the way.

We were all pretty good riders. We say today how we were all so crazy with the dare devilish things we tried, the jumps and the cliffs we attempted to ride on were definitely not the safest. Trust me we paid the price many times.

Many injuries later if we ever went for a ride today we would most certainly take the easy route down. We could go fast and keep up with each other, but most importantly we were all usually well prepared for anything along the way such as break downs or injuries. Greg luckily was excellent at knowing where we were going. It was as if he had an internal GPS. After hours of riding on trails we had never been on before he could always guide us back to the truck from just about anywhere. That was certainly a trait that we would learn to appreciate.

CHAPTER 3

THE TRIP BEGINS

S ummer of 1998 arrives. School is out, and work is slow. I have plenty of time on my hands to enjoy the outdoors. My brother Jeff is living in San Francisco, California and is now just about to move to Sacramento, California. Jeff is a few years older than me. At this point he had already moved out of our parent's house. In fact, Jeff had already moved more than a few times to and from different states. I'm sure I had lost count even by this point in time.

While living in San Francisco Jeff accepted a new job in Sacramento. He needed to move there in about a months' time. Jeff had called me up and asked if I would come help him move again. I say "again" because in the past I have flown out to help him move from one place to another.

In fact, the first time Jeff had moved away and out of our parent's house I recall being bummed out that he was leaving. It was a Monday morning and he was packing up his car. I had wished I could come along for the ride and help him with the move. Unfortunately, I was working every day that week. Jeff was moving to San Diego, California. He was planning on driving his car across the country. Early that morning as Jeff was getting ready to leave, I had been helping him pack some final things into his car. Jeff drove a small cramped two door BMW and oh did he think he was so cool in that thing. While helping him pack I thought, screw it, I am going with him. So I hopped in the car with him and we left for San Diego. Meanwhile I was supposed to be in work in a few hours so I called my co-worker Bill who turns out years later is actually a big Bigfoot buff.

Bill was a cool guy he could get along with anyone and we got along really well. I called him and said something along the lines of "Hey Bill I'm heading to San Diego and I am supposed to be at work all week. If anyone asks just say I am there, you saw me." Bill was the type that would just say ok no problem.

So a week goes by, I had driven to San Diego with Jeff. I also had a company cell phone at the time and I answered a few calls along the way pretending I was on an errand or something.

So I helped my brother move in, I flew home Saturday and back to work that Monday. Bill had obviously covered for me because nobody had known that I never showed up for work. I got paid for that entire week as well. I guess that goes to show how important that job was, but I was young so who cares. Bill ended up getting fired for some safety violation and I quit shortly after. Nevertheless, we actually ended up reconnecting years later at another job and I'll explain why that's relevant later.

When Jeff and I left for San Diego I was sad to see him move away but glad to spend some time with my older brother on the road trip. He knows how I like to explore places and he stopped along the way at some old ghost towns and a meteor crater, things like that. A ghost town though was probably as strange and as cryptic as I had ever gotten at this point in my life.

Jeff is also hilarious and definitely an oddball. He is very fun to be around so that's what propels me to come help him out or visit him from time to time.

Fast forward back to 1998. Jeff calls me and asked if I would come help him move to Sacramento. I said of course, and I then asked my friends Kenny and Greg if either of them wanted to come along.

Greg had just got his dream car, a 1969 Dodge Charger no more than a week earlier. He saved up all his money to buy that car so at this point understandably he was not about to go on an expensive trip but Kenny was all in though.

We planned our trip and headed out. We expected to be in San Francisco in just enough time to help my brother pack up and help drive his belongings up to Sacramento. Kenny and I also wanted to explore a bit so we actually landed in Las Vegas, Nevada. We were not old enough to gamble at that time but we thought it was still pretty cool being there on our own. We got a hotel room at the Riviera Casino on Las Vegas Boulevard. This casino was not the most extravagant hotel but it looked decent enough to us and it was in our price range. Plus, we had never been to Las Vegas before so we were fascinated with the place regardless.

We were on a budget and Jeff had asked us if we could rent a big SUV to help him move his stuff when we got there. Thankfully he said he would help pay for the rental car. We ended up with a Jeep Grand Cherokee. For about two days we hung around Las Vegas visiting sites such as the Hoover Dam and the Luxor Hotel. We both thought Vegas was very cool. We also went to the top of the Stratosphere Hotel that I believe was fairly new at that time. Mostly we explored the Fremont street section where there was live music playing outside. We liked this area so much years later we travelled back to Las Vegas on a few occasions when we could actually gamble and have some real fun.

Once it was time to head out and drive towards California we headed across the Mojave Desert towards Bakersfield and then out towards Morro Bay, California.

We had planned to visit some relatives in Morro Bay. When we arrived there we were impressed with this little town as well. The area was very nice; I remember visiting this huge rock right along the coast of the town. It was massive and quite the site to see, it was a rock sticking out of the ocean but close enough you can drive to. It was a picturesque little town almost resembling a small fishing village. This area would certainly be a great place to relax and retire that is for sure.

After we visited with family we were then off towards San Francisco. We managed to stop at a few more spots along the way such as the Hearst Castle which we were absolutely blown away with. We also drove through an area called 17-mile drive along the California Coast.

Kenny and I were definitely impressed with California and how beautiful the coast was in the summer. We talked about how we would love to live there some day. On our ride up towards San

Francisco I think we mostly chatted about grand ideas of moving there in a few years, not realizing how expensive it was then, and still is to live in that part of the country.

After some time, we finally made it to San Francisco. Jeff was living in a nice apartment complex that was just a few years old but the cost of living in the city was growing and Jeff had an opportunity to make more money elsewhere. He could now live in an area that had a much less cost of living and rent was cheaper so he jumped on it.

Jeff had to be at his new job on the following Monday. I recall we got to San Francisco sometime on Thursday. We helped Jeff pack up over the next two days before we left.

At some point that Thursday we noticed Jeff had two mountain bikes. One was his and the other was left behind by a former roommate who was a good friend of Jeff's. For some reason he could not take it with him when he moved out and he told Jeff he could keep it. Jeff told us he was going to sell it for him but never got around to do so.

After packing up for most of the day on Friday, that afternoon Kenny and I decided to take the bikes out. We wanted to ride around the city to check the area out. The only things we knew to look for was Alcatraz and the House from "Full House."

Neither of us had ever been to San Francisco before so we were eager to explore the area for a bit and take a break from packing up Jeff's apartment.

We soon discovered we mostly walked our bikes because the hills were excruciating to ride. Although the downhill areas were a blast. We explored some areas such as Fisherman's Wharf and Lombard Street. We also got to see Alcatraz from the top of one of the hills.

Later that night we met back up with Jeff and his friend Danny. We went out to grab some dinner. I remember Danny had come over in this crazy loud 1967 Camaro that he and his dad built. I only know that they built it because he talked about his car most of the night. He was obsessed with it to say the least. This guy was funny and he made us all laugh throughout the night. He talked with incredible sarcasm about everything. He and Jeff were a lot alike it was undeniably a fun time. We finished dinner and went home for the night.

Saturday morning arrived and Danny came back to help with some final things. We could hear him revving his engine outside at probably 6 o'clock in the morning. Danny brought us a quick breakfast, maybe donuts. He also gave us a half opened 12-pack of Mello Yello. I remember Jeff making fun of him for giving us a half opened package of soda for our ride, it was as if he just grabbed something from his house.

We loaded up Jeff's car and our rental Grand Cherokee and then headed off towards Sacramento. Other than the Jeep not starting after getting gas at a pit stop and then finally starting up ten minutes later or so, the rest of the trip towards Sacramento was much less dramatic and we managed to make it with all Jeff's gear intact.

CHAPTER 4

MOVING BOXES

We arrived in Sacramento probably two hours later on Saturday morning. The three of us basically spent the next two days setting up Jeff's new apartment. We connected the TV and video game, DVD, and stereo systems up. We organized the kitchen and so on. The new apartment complex was very nice, this place was fairly new as well. I admired Jeff, he moved out, he was on his own, had a good job and was living in a nice place. This place had a large pool, gym, and courtyard area. He was doing well for himself, I saw that and look up to Jeff. I wanted that for myself someday too.

Kenny and I knew Jeff was starting his new job on Monday morning and that he was going to be mostly busy for the next few days. We were not due to leave for Boston until the following Sunday, so we decided to check out the area over the next couple of days before we had to go. We actually got a few ideas from an old California travel style magazine that we found when packing up Jeff's things.

Since we had crammed the bikes in the back of the Jeep along with Jeff's things, we came up with the idea of doing one of our mountain bike exploration trips.
We didn't know the area, we had never been there before never mind mountain bike any of the trails but we didn't care. Any hiking trail would do and we always seemed to find something along the way

that worked out. Finding a new place we had never been to before was always part of the fun.

We read about an area called Mount Shasta that was probably about three hours North of Jeff's apartment. Three hours away was nothing in comparison to all the driving we had just done the previous week. When we went looking for trails with Greg we always drove far North up into Maine and New Hampshire looking for trails, this was no different.

Now at this point I did not tell Kenny but secretly I wanted to pick Mount Shasta as our destination. In fact, I insisted on it. I had noticed on the map in the article that on the way up there we would be passing through a town called Red Bluff.

My old girlfriend Kimberley from a few years prior had moved out from Boston to Red Bluff, California to live with her Aunt and Uncle. Honestly I was not sure if I would ever see her again but we were great together. Unfortunately, we lost touch once she moved away.

It was a total coincidence that I noticed Red Bluff on the map. After we agreed on Mount Shasta I did then mention to Kenny that since we were heading up that way we should stop in and see if we can find Kimberley. Kenny knew her too, in the years previous to this we all hung out together up until the time she moved away. She used to come watch us skateboard for hours. Kenny was always up for anything so we decided to try to find her.

After getting Jeff's computer set up we logged onto America Online internet service. We asked around to some of Kim's old friends until we were finally able to track down her phone number.

The next morning on Monday I called the number, I believe I spoke to her Aunt when I asked if Kimberley was home. She was not around but I left a message saying I was in town visiting. I left my cell phone number hoping she would get back to me in enough time to visit her on our trip up towards Mount Shasta.

That morning maybe an hour after getting our bikes ready and then eating some breakfast we started to make our way up north. We had bought a small fold out map book at a convenience store along with some things to add to a backpack we had also borrowed from Jeff. We had purchased a couple candy bars, some bottles of water and I had a couple cans of Mello Yello that Danny gave us a few days earlier. We also had a couple items that Jeff had with the bikes such as a tire patch kit and some bike tools along with a small first aid kit.

Back home when we would go mountain biking at least one of us would always bring along a backpack that was full of repair items. We have made the mistake one too many times of getting a flat tire or a broken bike chain only to have to walk the bike for miles to go home or back to the truck. We got into the habit

of being well prepared for all of our
mountain biking trips or so we thought...

CHAPTER 5

INTERSTATE 5

So when we finally hit the road it was pretty much one highway all the way up towards Mount Shasta. We would be passing right through Red Bluff. Although on our way there we ended up just driving right through the town because at that time I had not heard back from Kimberley yet. I think I had chalked it up to thinking she was probably not interested in talking to me, or maybe she had a boyfriend or something to that affect, nevertheless we continued on.

Our minds though were focused on mountain biking and until the Red Bluff area we were kind of concerned. Concerned about the surrounding landscape. As I mentioned we had never been to the area before and so far the land seemed pretty flat and rural. There was a lot of farm land and this was not exactly mountain biking territory.

It was not until we got passed the town of Redding, California that we started to really see some hills and some mountainous areas. At this point we still had about an hour left to go until we made it to Mount Shasta.

As were arriving to our destination we had no idea what we were in for. We had wondered if there would be trails or if it was possibly a ski resort; we really had no idea. We later managed to find a road that was incredible to drive on and the views were simply amazing.

We were able to drive very high up in elevation on this winding road before it eventually turned into a dead end.

We had to turn around but we were surprised at how close to the snow line we could get. This area that we were at was above all, stunning. The surrounding area seemed vast with enormous hills and mountains. From up on that road we could see this mountainous region we were in go on and on for what looked like eternity.

We hadn't really determined yet where to stop and get the bikes out and we were both so astonished at the scenery that we probably drove around for another hour or so. Although we loved the outdoors and the beauty of the forests that we were usually familiar with, we took some extra time to appreciate this new landscape.

It was possibly about 1:45pm at this point and we were now eager to get on

the bikes so we finally settled on a spot to pull off.
We pulled off to the side of the dirt road that we were traveling on. This and other roads seemed to go on and on for miles with nothing around other than the dense forest.

After driving away from the town on that dirt road we came up to an adjacent access road that had a gate on it.
The road didn't seem to be someone's property but it looked more along the lines of an old state access road. The road was overgrown with weeds, we assumed it was most likely used by patrolling forest rangers in the past. We didn't drive that far from the town it seemed, but we did venture away into a remote location. We did not see any other vehicles or forest rangers in the area. We didn't really think much about it at that time either. It's only now that we think about how we were pretty dumb to just wander off into an unfamiliar area. I've later read about the many people who have gotten lost in that area as well.

When we stopped we grabbed the bikes and the backpack from the back of the SUV. I was wearing a long sleeve shirt. I took that off and threw it into the Jeep. The weather was perfect for a bike ride, the sun was shining and the temperature was warm. We were both wearing a T-shirt and shorts, the weather was undeniably perfect for a mountain bike ride. If I could guess it was about 75 degrees.

CHAPTER 6

THE RIDE

We start to ride up the dirt road when we noticed what looked to be a few trails here and there. Possibly hiking trails but nothing really stood out. We pulled into a few trails only to find they sort of vanished into brush so we made our way back onto the road a few times. Finally, we found what appeared to be a nice clearing that led up towards a mountain side.

At this point we were still on somewhat flat land. The mountainous terrain had just now started up in this area. The dirt road we drove down was somewhat flat in comparison. We wanted to ride near the mountains but at the same time try to ride on some sloped long distance trails that looped along the side of the mountain as opposed to trying to mountain bike uphill all day. Let me be clear, this place was massive, it was not as if we could actually ride up Mount Shasta or any of the surrounding mountains.

As I mentioned we were probably a few miles from the town and the base of the mountain by the time we finally picked a spot away from the people and crowds.

We had hoped for some decent trails that might have some uphill and some downhill spots. We looked for trails typical of what we are used to in New England.
As we rode on we must have been riding for probably two hours and we loved

being in this area. We knew we didn't have anywhere else to be and neither of us was in a rush to leave. We were doing what we loved to do.

Now perhaps because it was a Monday or maybe Mountain Biking was not very big out here at the time, or maybe it was just because this area was somewhat remote, but we had definitely felt alone out there.

We had purposely driven away from the base of Mount Shasta for that reason; to be away from the people.

As far as mountain biking goes, the trails were excellent but at the same time it was kind of eerie. At one point when stopping to take a drink from our water bottles we commented to each other about how surprised we both were that there wasn't any other people around. Back home in the woods near our neighborhood we are typically used to sharing the trails with many hikers. The hikers usually yelled at us for being on the trails, as if they were for hiking only. They say we are ruining the trails with our bikes. However, there was none of that here. The trails seemed to go on for miles and miles, crisscrossing other trails along the way. But at some points the trails did seem to randomly fade into nothing at which point we were just riding looking for a trail to pick back up.

It was possibly the excitement of the easy to ride and fast trails but we found ourselves mostly riding downhill.
I wouldn't say they were "downhill trails" as some riders would call it but the majority of the time we seemed to be going away from the mountain side into some valleys.

We had hoped we could loop back around somewhere later. Somewhere that could bring us back to where we started. We had never stopped to find any trail maps and the map we bought at the store was just for roads. We actually left that map back in the Jeep and that ended up being big mistake.

I think it was just the eagerness to get going that we never thought it might be useful.

Although we had ventured off into the unknown woods before, this time was certainly different and unfortunately we did not have Greg's sense of direction this time. We had stopped for some sips of water along the way both expressing how fun the ride was and how we wished we had this back home. At times these trails were easy to ride and smooth and other times very rocky, unfortunately rocky trails really do beat up on these bikes.

Mountain bikers know when you're riding along there is a certain ping sound that a tire makes when a rock pierces and punctures a tire and the inner tube. You instantly know you have a problem. You just got a flat tire.

Typically, it's no big issue for us because we always travel with a patch kit but at that moment I heard that sound. My rear tire popped and we weren't exactly sure how far we were from the jeep, or where we were in general for that matter.

We never felt nervous or anything though because this was fairly common and had happened many times before. It's just sometimes a concern about getting the bike working again so we do not have to walk it back. Luckily we had the backpack and a tire patch kit.

CHAPTER 7

THE PUNCTURE

Back home we always said "let's just go for a ride and try to get lost." We all knew that we wouldn't fall off the face of the earth. We knew that we would most likely end up on a road or somewhere in which we could find out where we were. We probably egged each other on saying things like that to go further out into some of the trails. Plus, not being too far from the city at times typically we would always end up at a place that we do recognize. A trail would dump out onto a road or behind a shopping mall, odd places. But getting lost for a minute at times was all part of the adventure I suppose.

This however was different; we were in a place that we were both very unfamiliar with. We definitely realized that we were alone and away from people, it didn't seem as if there were any shopping malls around the bend that's for sure. At times the trails even thinned out to the degree that we were just riding in between trees. Fortunately, some areas were open enough to do so.

There we were, we were now stuck on a trail with a flat tire. I flipped my bike upside down so that I could work on it. If you have ever worked on a bike you know putting it upside down while resting it on the handlebars and the seat is an easy way to fix things. This gave me access to remove the rear tire. Thankfully we had the patch kit. There was also a tire pump attached to the frame, the kind that bolts in under the water bottle cage. I then start to unscrew the tire quick releases and unclip the brakes. I pull the chain off the rear cogs and as I pull aggressively on the tire to get it out from the frame my water bottle that was in the holder and was now hanging upside down had jiggled loose from me pulling on the tire.

The trail we were riding on was somewhat rocky and we had stopped on a bend. To the left of us the trail continued on slightly uphill and curved further around the bend. In front of us was a drop off getting gradually steeper towards the bottom. It was perhaps twenty-five feet down or so. To the right of us the trail continued slightly downhill around the bend.

At this point Kenny was sitting on the ground with his bike upside down as well. He was attempting to adjust some gears that had not been working properly.

As my water bottle jiggled loose it hit the ground and bounced off a few rocks.
It started to gain speed as it rolled down the trail. At first I just tried to kick it to the side since I had my hands full with the bike tire. The bottle had then started to roll towards the side of the trail that had the steep drop off. I quickly jumped up to run over and grabbed it before it fell down the slope. The bottle had rolled about seven or eight feet away from me. As soon I reached down to catch the bottle I hear a tree branch break from what seemed to be right behind me. I looked up and just down the trail at about ten feet away was what could only be .... Bigfoot. It was staring at me and it almost looked terrified as it slowly moved behind a small thin tree. I reacted as if it was a bear, all I could think about was how I should be still and quiet. This however, was no bear. It was nothing I have ever seen before. This was without a doubt one hundred percent Bigfoot!

Kenny had sensed something going on then said "hey what's up?" I motioned with my hand to walk over, while also motioning a second time I put my hand out to come over very slowly. Kenny then begins to walk over, tip toeing quietly and slowly until he was close enough to peek around the corner bend. His vision at first is blocked by the rocks and tree roots but as he slowly makes his way down the trail and around the bend he saw Bigfoot standing there behind the tree. We were quietly but absolutely freaking out, whispering "HOLY SH*T!" We had no idea what to do next, we didn't know if we should move backwards or run away. We didn't say it but I think we both knew that we shouldn't run since we had no idea where we were. Also we were both equally scared. We both thought if we ran that it might run after us, we didn't know if it was dangerous or how it would behave.

CHAPTER 8

MEETING BIGFOOT

We stood there for what was probably just a few minutes, both of us looking at Bigfoot and Bigfoot looking at us but I will tell you this, it felt as if we were all standing there for hours.

So let me explain what we saw. From about ten feet away we could tell this thing was probably seven to eight feet in height. Kenny is just over six feet tall and this thing seemed as if it had to be a good one to two feet taller. At that time, it was tough to say exactly how tall because it was downhill from us, later we determined it to be roughly 7'5" tall. It had gorilla type features but also human traits as well. It stood up on two feet its entire body apart from areas around the face, toes and fingers were covered with a reddish tinted brown hair. I hate to say it but this was close to your typical looking Bigfoot you see in the TV shows and very close to the Patterson-Gimlin Bluff Creek film. Up close you can see human emotions in its eyes and face but with a gorilla looking structure. It was certainly nothing we have seen before and this was no bear. It did not have a scary face. In fact, we had both thought it was a rather younger looking Bigfoot for some reason. We also thought it was somewhat curious because it was not running away from us. I have to say we were also grateful that it was not running towards us to attack us either.

We had started to slowly back up around the bend until the Bigfoot had awkwardly tossed some sort of chain from behind the tree at us.

The chain landed roughly four feet from us. I remember thinking, what the hell is this thing doing? Wondering if it was trying to lure us towards it. We both took a step forward and reached down very slowly to pick it up, keeping an eye on Bigfoot. When I got a closer look at the object. I realized it was a car keychain with a Volkswagen logo on it. The keychain was obviously old and distressed and it was something Bigfoot evidently found in the woods and was carrying for some reason.

This is going to sound crazy but I handed Kenny the keychain and as he takes a look at it he speaks to Bigfoot asking "Did you find this?" I know it sounds crazy and silly but put yourself in our shoes at this moment, what do you do? Bigfoot oddly seemed as if he knew Kenny was speaking to it but clearly it could not comprehend what Kenny was saying.

We had no idea what to do and this thing was now obviously as scared of us as we were of it.

Our curiosity had started to take over at this point and Bigfoot was still hiding behind a small tree. The tree only took up maybe one-third of its body so we could clearly see most of Bigfoot's figure. It reminded me of a shy child that might be hiding behind their parent's leg when other grownups are around.

Of course we did not speak the Bigfoot language if there is one. We found ourselves trying to lure it over to us speaking in a gentle tone like you would do to a child or a cat or dog.

We were only in the woods for a bike ride so we unfortunately did not have a camera or anything to capture this moment and cellular phones did not seem to have a camera on them at that point, at least mine didn't anyway.

After a few minutes of attempting to lure out Bigfoot from behind the tree we actually thought we were making some progress as it was taking a step or two away from the tree. Moving slowly backwards and towards the left it was now clearly visible with no obstructions.

Kenny had suggested that we should try to give it something to eat. He took a few steps back towards my bike and reached down and grabbed the backpack that we brought along with us. Inside it we had a couple candy bars. I recall we had some Milk Chocolate Hersey bars and possibly some BarNone bars if those were still around at the time, those were my go to candy bars back then. We are both pretty sure it was the Hersey bar that we had opened up. We both broke off a couple of chunks and ate some while it was watching us. After trying to make it obvious this was food I tossed the chocolate bar on the ground just a few feet in front of the tree and sure enough after a minute or so this thing had slowly moved forward and bent down to the ground, bending both knees as a human on two legs would do. It had proceeded to grab the candy while still watching us as it picked the candy up. It had then broken off a piece just as we had done and ate the candy.

We were both quietly snickering to ourselves but at the same time being careful not to scare or startle the Bigfoot. We remember saying something along the line as "Oh my god we are feeding a Bigfoot candy!"

Let me also reiterate at this point that both of us had almost certainly never mentioned Bigfoot to each other in our lives, neither of us has ever had anything to do with Bigfoot or anything Bigfoot related in our lives either.

I guess Bigfoot is just something that most people seem to know about. Some years later I saw a gorilla eating candy at a zoo it was strangely similar but still not the same. We both knew this was no gorilla. It is strange neither of us ever said "Is that a Bigfoot?" Yet we both knew it was a Bigfoot. We also knew we were witnessing something magnificent.

We had just watched Bigfoot eat a candy bar in almost one bite, faster than anyone I had ever seen eat candy. All we had with us was some candy bars, two Mello Yello soda cans and some bike tools in our bag. The little water we had left with us was in our water bottles. We both thought why not try to see if Bigfoot will drink some Mello Yello. I grabbed a can from the bag, it was warm and it had been shaking around in my bag for a while during our ride so I recall opening it ever so slowly just in case it started to spray everywhere. It foamed up slightly but I took a sip, Kenny then took a sip and then he slowly walked up a few feet and placed it down on the ground. As Kenny backed up towards me we both then backed up a couple feet to give Bigfoot some room.

Again we started to talk to it as if it were a child, saying "go ahead its ok". Bigfoot sure enough after a few minutes slowly moved forward while sort of crab walking a step or two since it was still in a sitting stance but just with bent knees, and not fully sitting on the ground. It reached out to grab the can of Mello Yello almost crushing it while picking it up. Half the soda was spilling out all over its hand and then it started to drink it just as we had done, though mostly dripping the soda all over itself.

Remembering this story now in preparation for this book we had joked saying, imagine if we had a camera and this was a YouTube video, what a great advertisement this would be for Mello Yello. I know it sounds funny today, but at that time being scared, yet ever so curious, these were the best ideas we came up with to prevent it from hurting us or running away. As some time goes by we discovered this may have actually helped. Bigfoot seemed to be more and more at ease with us.

I don't know if I would go as far as to say Bigfoot had let its guard down a bit because we were not posing to be a threat. But it did seem to be less nervous with us at this point and as time went by it was even more at ease with us.

Bigfoot was still in the same position, knees bent and was now starting to look around for the first time. Its eyes were now moving and not staying locked on us. Kenny and I had both just watched this thing in awe of what was happening. A few minutes had gone by while watching this Bigfoot look around with curiosity. We look back on it now wondering, was it hearing things that we couldn't hear? It was obviously very aware of its surroundings.

I'm not sure if we thought about this back then while we were in the moment. But because we were so curious of Bigfoot we didn't take notice that it may have been doing the same thing to us as we were doing to it. What I mean is it may have tried to see how we reacted when it threw the keychain towards us. We did react, we reached down and grabbed it. Just as we had done with the candy and the soda to see how Bigfoot would react.

CHAPTER 9

FOLLOWING BIGFOOT

After a few minutes or so Bigfoot then finally stood up and started to walk up the ledge above the bend we were on. Walking away opposite of the steep slope. As it began to walk away it was looking back as if it wanted us to follow along. Once again we are both thinking, what do we do? One of us had said, screw it lets go and follow.

We both followed behind Bigfoot roughly twenty feet or so behind. At this position we got to really see this thing and its body move. It never made any verbal noises or groans and it just looked back every few seconds perhaps to see if we were still following along. I remember wondering, if it wanted us to follow it, or is it trying to get away. We talked about it as we followed along asking each other if this was a good idea to keep going. Kenny had remarked that it was so big if it wanted to get away if could probably run so fast out of our sight.

As we walked along trailing behind we could see that this thing was muscular like Arnold Schwarzenegger but just covered in all hair. We could never really tell if it was female or male but what we did know was this thing was enormous and unlike any person or animal we had ever seen. It had to weigh maybe four or five hundred pounds. It was so apparently heavy that at some points you could hear a thumping noise that certain areas in the terrain made as it walked by.

You may have heard the term Skunk-Ape which is another name for a Bigfoot in the southern region of the United States around Louisiana and Florida. I have read stories of some encounters involving the Skunk-Ape that will often speak of a foul smelling odor that Bigfoot gives off.

Kenny and I never recalled there being such a strong foul odor with this Bigfoot, nothing more than some bad body odor. Don't forget we were sweaty and dirty from mountain bike riding as well.

By now we must have followed this thing for what we later thought to be around a mile or so into the woods. We were getting anxious that we had left our bikes behind as well.

The only thing we had with us was our backpack that just had another candy bar maybe two, some bike tools, and another can of Mello Yello. I also had my cell phone that I had put inside the backpack as well. In my cargo shorts pocket I had my wallet, Bigfoot's keychain and the keys to the Jeep. Kenny was not carrying anything on him at the time.

We are still walking behind Bigfoot, this is now heavy brush, and we had wandered way off any visible trails or openings. This thing moved in and out of the branches, bushes, and trees as if they had no effect on its body whatsoever. Kenny and I were having a hard time just keeping up. Having to move away branches and bushes to get through was a real struggle. We were getting scrapes and scratches all over our legs and arms.

After what was a strenuous walk for us, Bigfoot had finally stopped over by a pile of arranged fallen tree logs in a small clearing. There must have been about a dozen tree logs in the pile. The logs had obviously been placed together. They could not have fallen and rested in this position. These were fallen trees and almost all the branches had been broken off. They were piled together almost like someone had arranged them on purpose, they were stacked in a triangle formation.

There was no question that we were in the middle of nowhere yet there were no traces of machinery that could have placed them in the manner they were positioned. You would have to be very strong to move and lift these logs, we couldn't speculate as far as to say Bigfoot arranged these but it was unusual to say the least.

We were long off the hiking trails and into some dense forest. Bigfoot moved some rocks that had been pushed up against the logs, it looked as if there was a collection of items there.

We never got close enough to identify all the items. We moved in to within ten feet or so for a slightly better view of the items. If you were just walking by you would probably mistake it for a pile of trash someone left behind. But we felt as though Bigfoot had found these items around the woods and was then collecting them and bringing the items back to this location.

As Bigfoot was moving rocks and these things around it was now totally focused on the items and not so much us anymore. It had carried the crushed empty Mello Yello can during the walk the whole time and then placed it into the pile.

Some of the items we could see were an old hat, it was a baseball style hat that was green in color, olive green or possibly just faded green. There was also two or three brown and green glass bottles that resembled beer bottles. The bottles were old looking and without labels. There was also some sort of reddish fabric that looked as if it was an old worn and ripped t-shirt. There were definitely other items in there but our view was obstructed by the rocks Bigfoot had moved.

We never knew if Bigfoot brought us there to show us those things or if it was just our curiosity that made us follow along, but Bigfoot was not bothered by us being there and it was now totally transfixed on the items.

Years later we thought, did Bigfoot have the intelligence to think the soda was a gift and the can was something it could keep? And also was that act what made it want us follow it to that location of the collection? It was all very strange once we looked back and thought about it.

We stood by watching Bigfoot moving the items around behind the rocks, its back was slightly turned towards us and we had moved up against a hill of rocks and tree roots to get a better view. We had watched this thing for maybe twenty minutes or so. At this point we wondered what we were going to do now. Bigfoot was not paying attention to us in fact it was as if we were watching a child play with some toys, but in reality it was Bigfoot playing with a bunch of junk people had left in the woods.

I had whispered to Kenny that it was getting late in the afternoon and we have no idea where we are or how to get back to the Jeep. Plus, I still needed to go back and fix my bike.

I asked him what he thought we should do. We were both amazed but, how long could we possibly stay there. Kenny had agreed that we should leave but said something along the lines of we can't, or we shouldn't leave, this is too much of a miracle to miss seeing. I had agreed and trust me I knew myself that this was something significant to witness.

A few minutes later Kenny had started to move around. He was slowly walking away from the hill, motioning for me to come with him so we could get a better look. As we moved around the tree logs were now blocking more of our view of what Bigfoot was doing but we could see its face and eyes better.

Bigfoot still was not making any eye contact with us as we were moving around. Kenny had said to me "I wonder

if we should give him the backpack" and I was asking him, why, for what? Why would we do that? Kenny had thought that because he collected these things he found maybe he could carry a bag.
You can see where Kenny's love for animals comes into play. I thought Kenny was crazy because I didn't think Bigfoot would understand what it was for. I recall joking, "What is Bigfoot going to walk around the woods with a backpack on, drinking a Mello Yello while cleaning up people's trash?!"

Kenny was persistent on leaving the backpack so he grabbed my cell phone out of the bag and tossed it over to me. He then started to try to get Bigfoot's attention and showed it the bag while picking up some sticks and putting them into the backpack then taking them back out.

I felt Bigfoot sort of understood what he was doing but I still recall saying something like it was never going to use that. Kenny had then tossed the backpack over towards Bigfoot, it reached over to pick up the backpack and to my astonishment had then put something in the bag, and we assumed was the red t-shirt.

Our vision of the items was blocked by the logs but we could see the motion of its arms actually putting some things into the bag. We remember Bigfoot holding onto that Mello Yello can consistently though, hardly ever putting it down.

Then all of a sudden we heard sticks breaking in the distance but getting louder and louder as if someone was running towards us through the trees.

We both look around really quick wondering where it was coming from, Bigfoot had jumped up first and had looked around too for the noise. Bigfoot was holding the backpack and then all of a sudden ran off out of sight. It ran so fast as if it was frightened and in a split second was gone through the trees. It made us frightened so we then ran off in the opposite direction. We were both yelling "faster, faster, what the hell was that?"

We must have run for a couple minutes into the dense forest scraping up our legs and arms again until we found ourselves far enough away from what was chasing us. We leaned against the side of a rock face trying to both catch our breath.

We asked each other what the hell that was and what either of us saw. I think we both ran thinking each other saw something. We both reacted and started running for our lives. We were already on edge with this whole experience and we felt one another knew why we were running away. I think it was just being there with Bigfoot that was making us tense, after hearing these noises we were definitely shook up.

CHAPTER 10

NOW WHAT?

Neither of us saw anything coming towards us, we both only heard the noises of tree branches breaking and brush moving. Then when Bigfoot ran, we reacted and ran away too.

We dusted ourselves off and tried to figure all this out. We knew we had to go back and find the bikes.

We looked around to get our bearings. Although we had been lost before back home this time felt different. Perhaps it was because we were on foot without the safety net of the bikes but for the first time I can remember we both felt concerned about our current situation.

We decided to slowly make our way back to the spot we all ran from. We thought maybe there could be some logging company or someone nearby. We knew it was a long shot though because there was no evidence of people anywhere in the area, just some oddly stacked up logs.

We discussed the possibility of there being another Bigfoot or perhaps a bear that we should be concerned about. Something was running at us and we figured if there was something scary enough to make Bigfoot run, it could possibly harm us as well.

We decided it was best to take it slow as we made our way back to the logs.

After a few minutes of walking we realized all the zigzagging we had done while running through the brush ducking under trees, we had totally lost our sense of direction.

We then walked in a few different directions, but each time we'd say to one another this cannot be the way back. We were usually so good at remembering our path but nothing was coming back to us.

We must have walked around for twenty minutes to a half hour just looking for the way we came until finally Kenny had said "I think we are lost!" That was probably the first time either of us had actually said it out loud.

Now for the first time ever we felt as if we were in real trouble. We still had not seen any people and we were not sure exactly which way and how deep we rode our bikes into the woods. We were so used to ending up on a road or finding signs that led to a park or a picnic area that in the past when we actually tried to get lost, we really knew we couldn't. If we did it was very temporary. Plus, to add to our fears Greg was not on this bike ride with us. He was probably the best at knowing the way. This time we were totally on our own.

We wandered around for what seemed to be an hour before we knew that it was just getting too late and we need to just find our bikes and forget the logs.
We needed to look for anything that resembled a rock or a tree that we passed when following Bigfoot. Unfortunately, we could not find anything familiar we recognized.

I think we were so mesmerized at what was going on and what we were witnessing while following Bigfoot, we never took notice of anything else.

The sun was now getting lower in the sky and the trees we were under were so tall and thick we couldn't tell how much daylight we had left, but we knew it was getting late. It was time to act fast.

At that point when we said we need to forget the logs and find our way back to the bikes it was pretty much right then that I had realized we had given the backpack to Bigfoot. The backpack had our bike tools and patch kit inside of it. I remember cursing at Kenny for coming up with a stupid idea like giving Bigfoot the backpack, but I shortly apologized I knew I had agreed and it was such a crazy situation neither of us were really thinking logically with what we were witnessing.

We had then come to the realization that when we find the bikes we are going to have to walk the bikes back to the jeep since we now had no tools to repair the tire. We started to think about how far we had come. We had figured we were riding for about two hours and moving pretty fast, so perhaps that was about a three hour walk. Plus, we walked possibly a mile or so away from the bikes to the area with the logs while following Bigfoot. We then ran for a few minutes away from

that area. Then we had been searching for possibly an hour for our way back. When we put that all together we didn't know if in that past hour we were getting closer to the bikes or possibly walking further away. The scenery was looking all so similar and with no visible target to follow we were disoriented to say the least.
Now we knew for sure we were in some deep trouble.

Thankfully Kenny had grabbed my cellular phone out of the backpack before handing it over. I had checked it probably a hundred times over that past hour and unfortunately could never get any signal. I had dialed Jeff's number, Kimberley's number but nothing was working.

I will never forget looking at that phone it was an old Nokia phone with the signal on one side of the screen with vertical bars up the side of the screen. The battery strength was on the opposite side with the bars going up the side as well. There were no signal strength bars and only one battery bar. This phone would last for a while with a low battery but just to be safe I powered it off to reserve battery life thinking that this phone was our only lifeline. I could power it back on from time to time to once again check for a signal.

As the late afternoon rolled on we continued to wander around for hours. We knew Jeff had no idea where we were and if we never showed up he would assume we just stayed up there to hang in the area. We had also told him that we might be gone for a day or so.

By now the sun had set and it was getting very dark, the weather early in the day was beautiful at maybe around 75 degrees. We were both in shorts and a t-shirt and it was now starting to get a little cold. We had no idea for sure what the actual temperature was late that day but it felt cold to us and we are from Boston. Luckily we had been moving consistently and running from time to time so we were not freezing or worried about hypothermia or anything that drastic. We had hoped it was not going to get much colder especially since we had come to the realization we would be stuck here spending the night in the woods.

Sun had set and the moonlight was coming out, I recall our eyes adjusting rather well even though it got very dark. We had focused on being stuck there for the night. Our mission now was to find our bikes in the morning.

We made a plan to find a spot and set up camp for the night. We found an area that had some small trees that we could easily bend over. Using a small tree, we found we could use its long thin branches to sort of tie it to another tree. We piled some sticks, branches and logs on top of it trying to anchor them in place. We created sort of a hammock that you could lean on as opposed to sitting in.

We had decided to take turns sleeping, if we could get any at all. For the most part neither of us did get any sleep and we found ourselves just talking about what we had witnessed and how incredible that it was.

We said to each other no one is going to believe this. We had talked about the day and what we knew about Bigfoot, and if either of us had believed in Bigfoot before this. I recall we both said something similar like we never thought about it one way or the other before that day.

Kenny had joked that I was going to have one hell of a story to tell Kimberley if we ever found our way out of there. We were obviously trying to make the best of the situation, we laughed saying if she didn't want to see me again before this she really wouldn't now after I told her this story.

CHAPTER 11

ON A NIGHT JUST LIKE...

We had previously spent nights in the woods back home, but that was always with high school kids who had keg parties or when we were just hanging out and getting away from the city. But this was unlike anything we experienced before. These woods were quiet but loud if that makes sense. Quiet with the void of anything man made, anything we were used to.

We never heard airplanes, highway traffic, or anything that was relatable to us. It was loud because the bugs and the animals came out and it was quite the experience when things settled down and we just sat there and listened to nature.

As the night rolled on we talked about telling this story to people. At first we thought we needed to call the news. We were discussing being rational about it though and what the people that we told would think about the story.

We thought about calling either the news or the police but then wondered what would they actually do about it?

We also discussed the Bigfoot we saw. As far as myself, Kenny, and probably most anyone would assume before that time, Bigfoot was just a made up creature so no one was going to take us seriously.

We both felt at that time that we absolutely needed to let people know about this. We needed to be believed, this is too incredible for people to ignore.

When I write this I know I refer to Bigfoot as a "thing", or "It" sometimes I'm not sure the best way to even describe it. I can't call this thing, a creature, or a monster because this thing, this Bigfoot seemed so gentle and nice that it just would not be fair.

At that moment that night while sitting there talking we had felt the same way. We thought what if someone did take us seriously and what if someone would come out here hunting for it and killed it. We didn't want that to happen.

Looking back now we thought people would take our story more seriously than the others because ours was real. We definitely thought our story would be more important, and if someone was searching for Bigfoot they would hear our story and go out there looking for it.

We were obviously young and naive to think someone had to listen to us just because our story is genuine.

We cared about the Bigfoot. I thought that we needed to be careful with who we tell this story to and maybe we shouldn't call the news because people might actually go out there hunting.

We discussed what to do throughout the night until the early morning when the sun had ever so slightly begun to light up the sky.

It was still mostly moonlight but we knew we had to get it together and find a way out of there. We had come up with a few ideas, we thought about trying to find the bikes or forgetting that strategy all together and just search for some people instead. But how do we do that? Easier said than done. After considering the fact that we had no repair tools to even fix the bikes when we found them. We finally agreed on ditching the bikes, unless we found a landmark that we recognized that could take us back to the bikes. We also agreed that we need to go uphill when possible and search for a vantage point to look for any sort of buildings or houses. Lastly we agreed that if we came across a river or a body of water that we would follow it down stream. We hoped that any of these scenarios would get us to some help, and eventually back to our Jeep.

CHAPTER 12

MOUNTAIN DEW

That morning, everything was damp from the cold moisture. It never rained that night but there was a lot of condensation in the air until the sun came out. Everything being damp sort of dampened our spirits as well. We were feeling pretty miserable by then. For what must have been a few hours, we walked around searching but never seeing or hearing anything that could bring us closer to anyone. We never saw anything that looked recognizable that might take us back to our bikes either. There were no trails, no trail markings, nothing. The whole area seemed unexplored. Apparently this was Bigfoot's territory and it made sense.

You may recall the trails that we were traveling on while riding our bikes were scattered and very sparse towards the end. At times I would say that they were not trails at all.

We found ourselves walking up hills and down. Both of us had attempted to climb up a couple trees but it was difficult and the forest was so dense that there was just nothing to see. Plus, we were battling some morning fog until the sun could clear things up.

The day rolled on, I checked my phone turning it on and off a few times and never could find a signal. We walked for hours and hours taking breaks to sit and relax a bit. We were both exhausted from

the bike ride, plus we were both going on no sleep, and no food.
The forest seemed to just go on forever. We walked for countless miles, more than either of us had ever done previously in our lives.

This area was very rocky and mountainous it was hard to traverse. At times when we could see through some clearings the entire area looked like a mountain valley. There were no buildings, houses to be seen, we looked for water towers, antennas; there was nothing.

So far this day we were both feeling hopeless and weak. The temperature was warm and the weather was nice again, but we were hungry and tired. While walking along at a time when we were both very quiet and just thinking to ourselves Kenny had stopped still. I said "what?" He pointed and said to look at the slope we had come up to. It was an incline that looked as if it went straight up. Steeper then what we had been coming across. We made the decision to hike up the steep terrain as far as we could go. We were determined to find something off in the distance. On the way up we talked about how there must be rivers coming down from the top of Mount Shasta. When we drove up the winding road in the Jeep we saw snow melting when we reached the snow line.

We considered the fact when we went looking for trails we knew we had driven back down from the mountain side and back across the highway into some deep woods. We thought perhaps we were too far away from any water source coming from the mountain but we knew we had to look. We thought for sure we might be able to at least see the tip of Mount Shasta and head back towards that direction.

For the better part of the afternoon and late into the day we finally made it to the top of one of the peaks we climbed. The temperature had dropped, we felt it was freezing up there.

We looked off into the fading sunset.
There was a hazy fog and overcast that
had rolled in plus it was getting dark so
we couldn't see Mount Shasta.

Looking down into the dark hills, we saw
mostly trees and deep green valleys. We
did see what we thought were headlights
off in the distance popping in and out of
sight. We assumed it was a road down in
one of the valleys. We had both discussed
how to get down to that area but also,
and most importantly, how we would
know we are walking straight towards it.
It was so easy to lose your sense of
direction in this area.

We knew we needed to make a decision
soon and go for it. We were both freezing
from the cold, we needed food, water and
rest, and we also did not want to spend
another night out there.

We had come up with an idea. On this
side of the mountain, although it was
dark, we could just barely make out that
the terrain slopped down into a valley.

The same valley where we saw the lights flickering through the trees.
Towards the left and the right side of the valley the trees sloped back up the sides, almost as if the ground funneled down towards the bottom. The very bottom of this spot was somewhat close in proximity to where we saw what we hoped was a set of moving headlights.

CHAPTER 13

THE DESCENT

We decided to go down a bit lower and either find a place to set up for the night, or just keep going. We didn't want to spend the night again and as we got lower and lower, we actually started to feel like we could breathe better and we were warming up. Perhaps it was the increased oxygen or the adrenaline of finding a way out but we decided to just keep going and going.

Our bodies were so beat up from hiking through brush, sliding up and down rock faces. We were both very dirty and full of scrapes and cuts but we quickly learned when there is the slightest bit of hope it's amazing what your body can do.

We both powered on and after a long night of walking, we finally made it to the bottom. At the bottom we ended up at a rushing river. We felt as if we had struck gold. We both immediately put our faces to cold water and drank that water as if it was the greatest thing in the world. We washed ourselves off a bit and discussed what our next move should be.

When we were up on the peak we had thought the headlights were over in a certain area to the right of us. We knew the spot we came down was not directly next to the lights we saw but we had an idea where to go. We had decided that heading down that river might bring us to where we may have seen the road with the vehicle.

Only moonlight could guide us as we
walked along a sandy creek bed full of
rocks and fallen logs. We walked and
walked until we finally saw an overpass
bridge that looked as if it had a road or
railroad tracks crossing the river.
We climbed up the side and at the top
was a road with an area people could pull
off and park, but there were no cars. We
knew we needed to get onto that road
when someone drives by.

We must have sat there on that road for
an hour, but strangely we already felt
rescued at this point. Our fears had
definitely subsided. It was familiar to us
to find a road we could follow. We kept
saying to each other that a car has to
come by here at some point.

Finally, we hear an engine, we then see
headlights coming around the bend and
through the trees. We both jumped up in
the street and flagged down a man in an
old GMC pickup. We ran up to his
window and told the man we were lost
and we had been in the woods for two

days, we lost our bikes and our way home. We must have been talking so fast, he just said to settle down and relax, and he would take us to where we needed to go. Our only problem at this point now was, we had no idea where we were and where the Jeep was.

The man pulled off into the parking area and told us how he has been traveling around that area for years he could help us retrace our steps. We honestly felt bad that this man was taking his time at this hour in the early morning to help us to this extent.

We asked him his name and where was he headed. He told us his name was Rusty. He explained to us that after he had retired he began traveling all around the United States playing in horseshoe tournaments. He was traveling on a long drive back home from a weekend tournament.

CHAPTER 14

RUSTY

The man told us he did not have any place to be anytime soon and he would be glad to help us. We explained how we pulled into town looking for Mount Shasta. When we realized how big the area was we pulled off and drove down some dirt roads until we found the right spot. We figured we could possibly find our Jeep if we went back to town and followed the similar course we took.

We hopped into Rusty's pick-up truck, it had a large bench seat, and as he drove us into town we told him all about our story from the beginning to the end. We actually think he believed us because he said he heard stories about Bigfoot before.

Rusty gave us some ham and cheese sandwiches that he had in a cooler. He said he always brought sandwiches along for his long drives. That had to be the best sandwich we ever had.

Once we got back into town we retraced our steps, following along the same dirt roads until it was just about the time the sun was coming up, we finally found our Jeep.

Rusty really helped us out and we will be forever grateful for what he did. We never got his full name, we wished we could have thanked him more for what he did to help.

I was so lucky I had put the key to the Jeep along with my wallet in my cargo shorts deep pocket and not in the backpack.

We got in and started up the Jeep, we both looked at each other like, are you kidding me... what just happened?!
We both just sat there laughed for a minute until we said let's go grab some breakfast and get the hell out of here.

We stopped at a small diner and ordered some breakfast. I turned my phone on and finally I had signal. Jeff had left a message asking where we were, but I didn't want to call anyone at that point. We both just wanted to sit, relax and eat a hot meal.

We finished up and paid. We left the diner and while walking out back to the car, Kimberley had finally called me back. She told me she tried to call a

couple times and explained that she was out of town for the past 2 days.
When I told her we were lost in the woods and had one hell of time trying to find our way out, she was definitely taken aback.

Kimberley said she wanted to meet up with us so she could see me again, also she wanted us to tell her what happened. I immediately agreed and Kenny was up for it so we told her when we get back down towards Red Bluff I would call her back.

On the way back to Red Bluff I called Jeff and told him we were heading back but stopping to see Kimberley and we will see him later that night. I remember thinking how excited I was to see her and also how I wished I could have cleaned myself up a bit first.

When we arrived in Red Bluff I called her back and we agreed to meet at a bowling alley. It was still early in the morning, the bowling alley was not opened yet.

Kimberley told us she would meet us there so Kenny and I waited in the parking lot.

CHAPTER 15

KIMBERLEY

Kimberley is younger than me and at this time she did not yet have her license to drive. When a bus pulled up to the bus stop adjacent to the parking lot I saw her getting off the bus to meet us. We both hurried towards each other. We hugged as if we were still in love and we were just waiting to see each other after a long weekend. But it had been years, although maybe that was the case. Perhaps we were still in love but we just didn't know it yet.

She asked what happened to us, and why we were both wearing dirty tattered clothes with cuts and scrapes all over our bodies. We were dirty and probably smelled bad but I think all that made her more interested in why we said we had gotten lost.

We sat in the parking lot and we told her the story from the very beginning to the end. How we met Bigfoot and how he was collecting things in the woods.
It was certainly at this moment hearing myself tell this story that I thought we sounded crazy.

If someone told me that story I would have laughed and called them crazy and I expected her to do the same. She didn't, she had a look I will never forget. It was a look that only she has ever given me when telling this story. She believed me. She was fascinated by what we had told her and she wanted to know every detail.

The three of us probably sat there for two hours just talking. It was really great to see her again. We had a relationship some years earlier and it was cut short when she moved away.

When you're young sometimes losing someone seems as if it's the end of the world, and other times you might not care. With Kim it was different when she left, somehow it never felt as if our lives would be apart. I think we felt it was almost like she was just moving to another town that was close by.

However we went our separate ways and we did indeed lose touch. Looking back now I know I had felt as if we would meet again in some point in our lives. When that day came it was as if we were never apart.

When the bowling alley opened up we went inside and played pool. We ended up hanging out for a couple more hours. We talked about old times and how we were all doing over the past few years.

When it was time to leave we drove her home to her aunt's house. We dropped her off, and she gave me a kiss and said to call her when I got home.

On the way back down to Sacramento Kenny and I talked about the crazy couple of days we had just experienced. When we reached Sacramento we told the story again to Jeff but it was received with much less fanfare then Kimberley expressed. It was probably because Jeff thought we were making it up and mostly because we lost his bikes. We told him Bigfoot stole his bike and rode off with it into the woods with his backpack.

A few days later we packed up and returned the Jeep and flew home from Sacramento to Boston. Kimberley and I had talked off and on throughout the years mostly online but there was very little communication between us.

We had moved on and started living our lives. Kenny and I remained friends but as life moved on we got jobs and had different relationships and priorities that kept us busy.

We told our story to a few friends, Greg, our parents of course, but we never really knew if anyone believed us. We never called the news, we never even spoke about calling the news once we got home. I guess it was just being in the moment that we thought it was the most important thing ever, but it was, it still is and we will never forget it.

I had gotten a full-time job working with Bill who I had worked with years earlier. One day Greg and I were visiting a car show in his Charger when I ran into Bill again, we got to talking about work and how funny it was when he covered for me years earlier. He was hiring people at his job so I joined him. It was probably a few years later that I told Bill about my Bigfoot story and he loved it. I had never known he was secretly a huge Bigfoot fan. It was actually Bill who encouraged me to finally write this story and to share it with people.

After about ten years or so, Kimberley and I had now totally lost contact. I had gotten different phone numbers over the years. I had moved out of my parents' house and she had move out from her aunt's house.

One day I get a call from a friend of mine saying Kimberley was looking for me, she was a mutual friend of ours and they had still been in touch randomly over the years. She then relayed me her phone number. Kimberley was now living in Arizona City, Arizona.

On this day I was actually back in California helping my brother move again down to Austin, Texas. I don't know how or why it was that I received that phone call at that time. At a time when I would soon be driving through Arizona on my way to Austin, Texas. Nevertheless I called her as soon as I could.

She had told she was watching TV one day when some sort of a Bigfoot research show came on and she could not stop thinking about me and my story.

She also wanted to see how I was doing and what I've been up to over the years. I mentioned that I was back in California and how our timing is always so strange but works out. I told her that the time when I met up with her ten years earlier I was supposed to go up there for a ride and head back down to Sacramento the same day.

I reminded her she was actually out of town for two days. With me getting lost it held me up there until she got back in time to call me. Now fast forward ten years later and here we are again.

I told her I will be driving a U-Haul to Austin, Texas and I will call her when I drive through. When I reached Arizona City we met up at one of the chain restaurants in the area and again it was as if we never skipped a beat. We could jump back into conversation like we never stopped.

My time there was short but we agreed to stay in touch and meet up again. She was coming home to Boston in a month or so for a wedding and I agreed to be her date.

After seeing each other back in Boston, I later flew out to Arizona a few times. We met in California once visiting Long Beach and Los Angeles as well. Every time we met we felt closer and closer until we finally decided to have a committed long distance relationship.

I never really told my Bigfoot story much after that first time getting back home from the trip in 1998. Kimberley was perhaps the only one I spoke to about it since. She was probably the only one who truly believed us and I was always grateful for that. In a weird way we always thanked Bigfoot for causing me to get lost because if we just had a normal ride and went home I may have never seen her during that trip and possibly never again.

After a year or so of traveling back and forth from Boston to Arizona, she decided to move back to Boston where we settled down and some years later got married.

I feel like these few days in the woods was a life changing event, in more ways than one. It was an amazing experience that led me to respect the outdoors, life, the unknown, love, friendship, family and friends and well,
I know now I owe it all to...
The Day I Met Bigfoot.

THE END.

ABOUT THE AUTHOR

My name is Craig Durham, I wrote this book because it brings me back to a time when I was young. A time before growing up paying bills and having real responsibilities.

I am sure if we could all go back and tell our younger selves to enjoy every second of it while it lasts we would do so in a second.

I can remember my father telling me "Don't get old son, enjoy your life."

Growing up I spent most of my time outside playing sports with friends, exploring the woods. You might call it, just typical kid stuff. Is it typical kid stuff anymore these days? Maybe it's just my neighborhood but it does seem as though kids do not play outside like my generation did. If I was inside all day my mother would say "what are you doing? Go outside and play it's nice out!"

Fast forward and now I have fond memories of the friends in my neighborhood, some of whom are mentioned in this book. I'm glad I grew up in a generation where we had to go down to the school yard to see if anyone was around, or ride a bike to a friend's house and see if they were home. I am also grateful that I have stayed in touch with many of them as well. Although time goes on, our lives get busy, I found myself thinking back to those days and realizing how lucky I was to grow up in a neighborhood full of great people and friends.

Of course there were a few old mean people in the neighborhood that hated us kids and the games that we played in the streets, but terrorizing them was equally as fun. It's all a part of growing up I suppose.

Sometimes I wish I could go back, but then I realize those people and the times we spent together made me who I am today. The eagerness to explore and look for interesting places growing up, I believe brought Kimberley and I back together.

We often talk about the way we got back together and how it's strange the way things turned out. Now we are both on an adventure together. I guess my point is... Try to enjoy life, the older we get it seems as if time ticks on faster and faster.

I try to slow it down by thinking of about the great times and memories like the ones mentioned in this book. So my advice, stay young stay active, explore the world if you can.

I mentioned today's generation and I wonder, are they missing out? Do they go out and explore like we did? Or do they just explore the worlds of online video games?! Nevertheless, maybe you're one of those youngsters, and if so, what are you doing reading this book, go for a bike ride or something will ya it's nice out!

ACKNOWLEDGMENT

I want to thank all my friends who participated in writing this book with me. Kenny you were a great help, it was exciting to sit down again for a few days and reminisce about all the details of this story. Greg I wish you were there for the road trip but if you did come you probably would have gotten us out of there in five minutes. Then I would not have met up with Kimberley back then and life would have most certainly turned out to be much different. Jeff I still owe you a bike I know. Kimberley thanks for always believing in me and coming along for the ride as we find new adventures together. And Rusty, wherever you are Thank You... you're probably off playing horseshoes somewhere right now eating ham and cheese sandwiches.

Oh and Bigfoot... You owe me a Mello Yello!

THANK YOU FOR READING

THE DAY I MET
BIGFOOT

BAYSTATE STUDIOS
BOOK PUBLISHING
BOSTON, MA

CONTACT INFORMATION
BAYSTATESTUDIOS@GMAIL.COM
FACEBOOK.COM/BAYSTATESTUDIOS